ALL SAINTS
MARGARET S[treet]

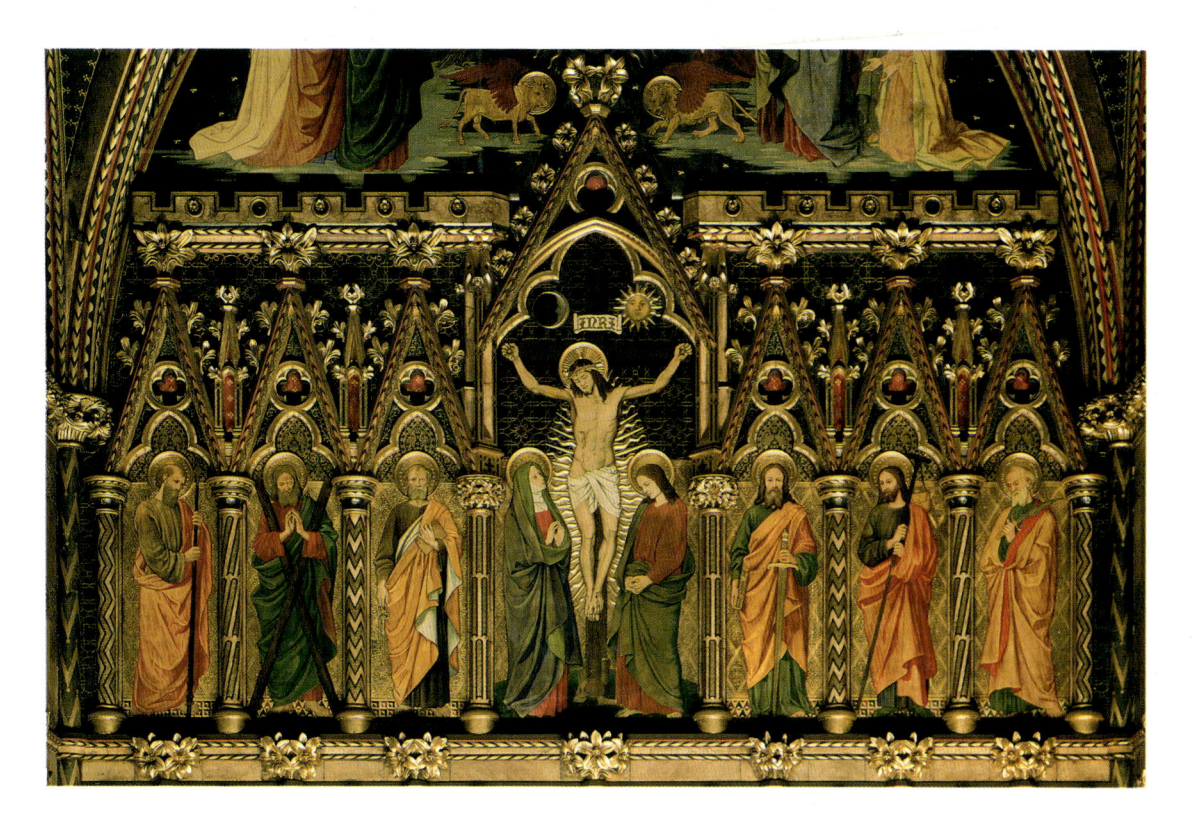

Vicar's Welcome

Variously described as 'an exotic and mysterious cavern' and 'a kind of parish church for the world', All Saints speaks eloquently of its architect's passion and resourcefulness. Hidden away in the less frequented streets adjoining Oxford Circus, the church is a place set apart and dedicated for prayer and praise. Our doors are open daily from 7 in the morning until 7 in the evening. The ministry we offer is one of simply 'being here' – a Ministry of Availability.

Above all we seek to express the joyfulness of the Christian Faith, a ready welcome and hospitality – a teaching and preaching ministry which extends far beyond the meagre parish boundary. Always a place of purpose and prophecy, All Saints stands in the last decade of the 20th century looking forward with faith and hope to the future. Here we hold together the paradox of glorious splendour as well as simple service to humankind.

Welcome! This is none other than the House of God. Be still and know...

DAVID HUTT
Twelfth Vicar

An Introduction

Visitors to All Saints frequently fall into one of two categories: those who make it a special object of pilgrimage through long association or as a result of another's recommendation, and those who stumble upon it by chance. The former have some kind of expectation, the latter rarely do. The immediate impression upon entering the door is that one has come to a place set apart. It takes a little while to accustom the eyes to the relative gloom – and then to come to terms with the proliferation of decoration. For some it is overwhelming and not readily understood.

Most visitors, however, experience a strange sense of awe and wonderment – and that is exactly what the founders set out to achieve, and what successive generations of vicars and congregations have consciously perpetuated by their self-giving and their prayers.

Much of what the Tractarian movement (see below) stood for has found its place in the parishes of the land to such an extent that few today would question the celebration of the Eucharist Sunday by Sunday, the regular recitation of morning and evening prayer, the provision of spiritual counselling, the

ABOVE: *Counselling and the Sacrament of Penance have long been vital and integral parts of the work of this church, where experienced priests are available every day for the Ministry of Reconciliation.*

RIGHT: *This is the centre panel of a triptych originally presented to the Margaret Chapel by Alexander Beresford-Hope. Recent examination has shown it to be a hybrid – this panel is believed to be early 16th-century Flemish but the wings are much later additions.*

LEFT: *After sharing in "The One Bread" at the altar, that fellowship is continued in refreshment and friendship in the courtyard.*

accord them today. All Saints was very much a flagship in this campaign, albeit without seeking the role – a conscious embodiment of deeply held principles, and as such, an extremely important church.

Within the Church of England it has provided a disciplined daily offering of prayer and praise to almighty God and at High Festivals or on Holy days resounded with all the glorious splendour of a rich inheritance. But unlike many other churches who were part of the movement for restoration of catholic privileges, All Saints has never been drawn Romewards for its inspiration. Cyril Tomkinson (Vicar 1943–51) once thus rebuked a visiting priest who asked for the use of a Roman Missal – 'the rule here is music by Mozart, choreography by Fortescue, decor by Comper, ... but libretto by Cranmer '.

Flagships today are out of fashion, yet All Saints continues to be loyal to its past and authentically eccentric. Much of what it stands for is valued by the considerable congregations and visitors alike as not only meeting aesthetic and spiritual needs but also pushing forward the conscience and the thinking of the church to engage with real-life situations. To this end clergy and laity alike sense this to be part of the strategy for the church of the future – respectful and grateful to the past but nevertheless deeply aware of God's moment now.

At the heart of our purpose is a spirituality of the incarnation and although we are profoundly grateful for a building of such unique quality and power in evocation, it is in the formation of Christian souls that our energies are directed. The Church, wherever it is to be found throughout the world, remains *people*. However small a Christian grouping may be, it is to the promise 'where two or three are gathered together in my name . . .' that we look.

sacrament of penance and reconciliation, or the easy engagement of the senses with colour, fabrics, ornaments and other aids to devotion. Yet 150 years ago this was not so. The catholic movement of the 19th century was instrumental in gaining for these elements of worship the acceptance we

Theology in Architecture

The origins of All Saints lie in the visions of one of the most remarkable and influential bodies to have existed in the 19th century, the Cambridge-Camden Society, founded in 1839 and known from 1845 as the Ecclesiological Society. Composed largely of romantic young idealists, the group set out to revive historically authentic Anglican worship and ceremonial, to restore medieval churches and to supervise the building of new churches. In 1841, they proclaimed a scheme for 'erecting . . . a Model Church on a large and splendid scale'. The church was to embody the deeply-held tenets of the Society:

- It must be in the Gothic style of the late 13th and early 14th centuries.

- It must be honestly built of solid materials.

- Its ornament should decorate its construction.

- Its artist should be 'a single, pious and laborious artist alone, pondering deeply over his duty to do his best for the service of God's Holy Religion'.

- Above all the church must be built so that the 'Rubricks and Canons of the Church of England may be Consistently observed, and the Sacraments rubrically and decently administered'.

Alexander Beresford-Hope, later M.P. for Maidstone and son-in-law of the Marquess of Salisbury, supervised and largely sponsored the project on behalf of the Ecclesiological Society. He chose the architect William Butterfield, who drew his first designs in 1849. Butterfield's ideas were often in conflict with those of Beresford-Hope and the antagonism between the two goes some way to explaining the discrepancies in the style and decoration of the church.

Butterfield's ingenious plan was dictated by the choice of site. The Margaret Chapel, built in the 1760s for a deist sect, had from 1839 been patronised by an eclectic Tractarian congregation, who wished to rebuild in a style more suited to a liturgy expressive of their principles. They agreed that the Ecclesiological Society should use the site for their Model Church, but this left Butterfield with an extremely constricted space within which to work. He had just over 100 feet square in which to fit a church, a choir school and a clergy house. His solution was to place the church at the back and bring the house and the school to the front, level with the street. The achievement is masterly.

BELOW: *Ground Plan of the church and vicarage in 1990.*

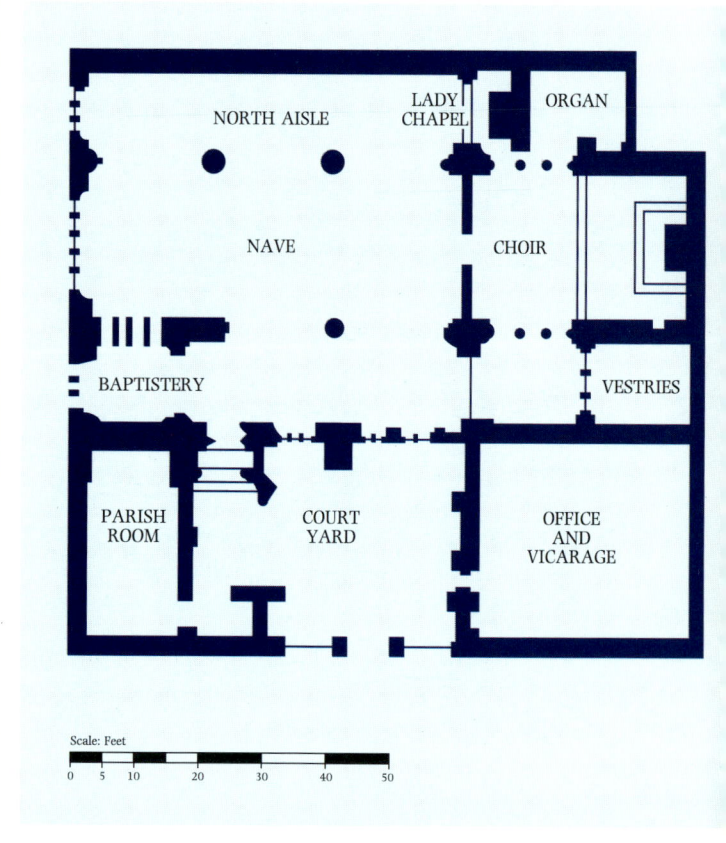

A drawing of the interior from the architectural journal,
The Builder, of 1859.

An Architectural Perambulation

The exterior of All Saints is seen to best advantage from the steps of 82, Margaret Street (All Saints House), opposite. The church and its associated buildings are in brick, a material originally abhorred by the Ecclesiologists who favoured rough stone walls and the 'rude hammer-dressed ashlar and rubble work of the ancient mode'. But by 1847, members of the Society had changed their minds. Having fallen under the influence of the churches of Italy and North Germany, they now proclaimed the virtues of brick. Butterfield himself felt a personal mission to 'give dignity to brick', and the pink brick he chose was more expensive than stone. The bold chequered patterning may owe something to Ruskin's advocacy of this style, but it is more likely to be based on English East Anglian tradition. The effect was certainly a far cry from the rural English model that the Camden Society had advocated just a few years before.

As we enter the courtyard, the first thing one sees is the great buttress with its relief carving of the Annunciation, symbolic of the Christian story. This was the only representation of the human form when the church was first built. It is placed off-centre, and leads the eye diagonally towards the porch and upwards to the tower and spire (which is based on the great spire of St Mary's Church, Lubeck).

On the right is the vicarage, which now houses the parish office as well, and on the left is the old choir school building, containing the parish room on the ground floor and residential accommodation above. The parish room was once the choir school refectory and contains the best remaining example of a fireplace of Butterfield's design, as well as his distinctive cast iron beams. On the north wall is a series of panels representing Christ and the four Evangelists.

RIGHT: *Given to the church in 1916, this picture is by the early Florentine painter, Bicci di Lorenzo (1373–1452) but has suffered much overpainting in the 19th century.*

BELOW: *A set of panels originally from Christ Church, Woburn Square (now demolished). They were painted as a memorial to Christina Rossetti by Thomas Rooke (1842–1942), an assistant to Burne-Jones. They are now on permanent loan to All Saints.*

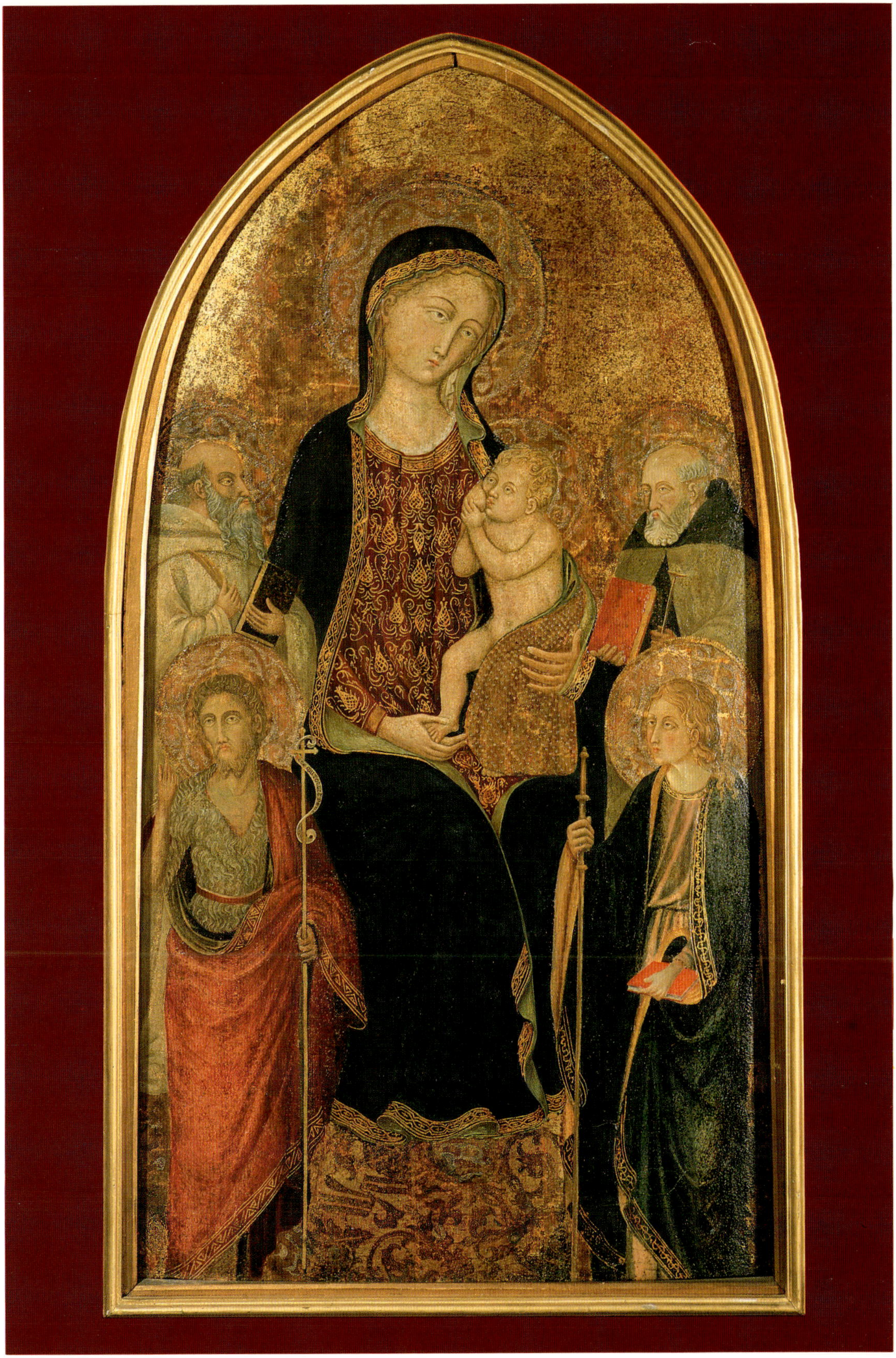

The Nave and Aisles

The interior of the church almost defies description. A riot of colour and patterning meets the eye, a great *Te Deum* of praise expressed in coloured tiles, brick, painting and gilding. The newcomer may find it difficult to take in all at once and at first the effect may appear discordant. But with further acquaintance it becomes apparent that the internal space is brilliantly handled.

The lavish decoration owes much to Ruskin who, in *The Seven Lamps of Architecture* (1849), had advocated the use of chequers, zig-zags, stripes and geometrical colour mosaic. Some of the detailing may have been taken from the plates in Matthew Digby Wyatt's *Specimens of Geometrical Mosaic of the Middle Ages* (1849). Significantly, both Ruskin and Digby Wyatt dismissed the use of tiles as opposed to stone and marble, making Butterfield's abstract use of colour and materials very much his own. Indeed Ruskin did not 'altogether like the arrangements of colour in the brickwork' and Beresford-Hope complained that Butterfield had treasonably 'spoiled his own creation with the clown's dress, so spotty, spidery and flimsy'. The critic C.L. Eastlake suggested in 1872 that 'there is evidence that the secret of knowing where to stop in decorative work had still to be acquired'. It is hardly surprising that in later life Butterfield wrote that 'the architect of All Saints does not lie upon a bed of roses'.

Colour and patterning is not restricted to the walls and the nave. Butterfield's tiled floor, made by Minton, is deep red with black checks and a white stone diaper, while the north and south aisles have a triangular variation of this pattern. The roof, now repainted, was originally in chocolate and white with blue detailing. The overall impact is extraordinary, and shows Butterfield as a master of abstract flat patterning.

The font is placed in the south-west baptistery and dates from 1857–8. Now vanished are the ironwork scrolls originally under the baptistery arch, admired by Gerard Manley Hopkins for the 'touching passionate curves of the lilyings'.

The large paschal candlestick standing near the font is a copy of one in the Certosa at Pavia in Italy.

The ceiling is decorated with 'the Pelican in its Piety', the bird piercing its breast to feed her young. The motif is symbolic of the Fall and Redemption of man, for the pelican was supposed to slay her rebellious offspring then revive them with her own blood.

Butterfield's brilliantly coloured pulpit of 1858 or thereabouts is one of his most remarkable achievements, an excellent example of the geometrical colour mosaic that Ruskin so favoured.

The nave altar is made of oak and is used daily at the lunchtime Eucharist intended primarily for those employed locally. It is a memorial to David Sparrow (1938–81), tenth vicar of All Saints (1976–81).

RIGHT: *The nave from the north-east corner. The arcade has shafts of Aberdeen granite, with capitals of Derbyshire alabaster, based on the foliage corbels at Warmington Church, Northants.*

BELOW LEFT: *The font, a gift from the Marquess of Sligo, is of Derbyshire grey marble inlaid with other marbles and carrying carved angels bearing shields. The original pyramidal oak and brass cover has disappeared.*

BELOW: *Butterfield's pulpit cost £400 at the time of its construction (£40,000 in today's terms). It incorporates Derbyshire fossil grey, red Languedoc, yellow Sienna and Irish green marbles.*

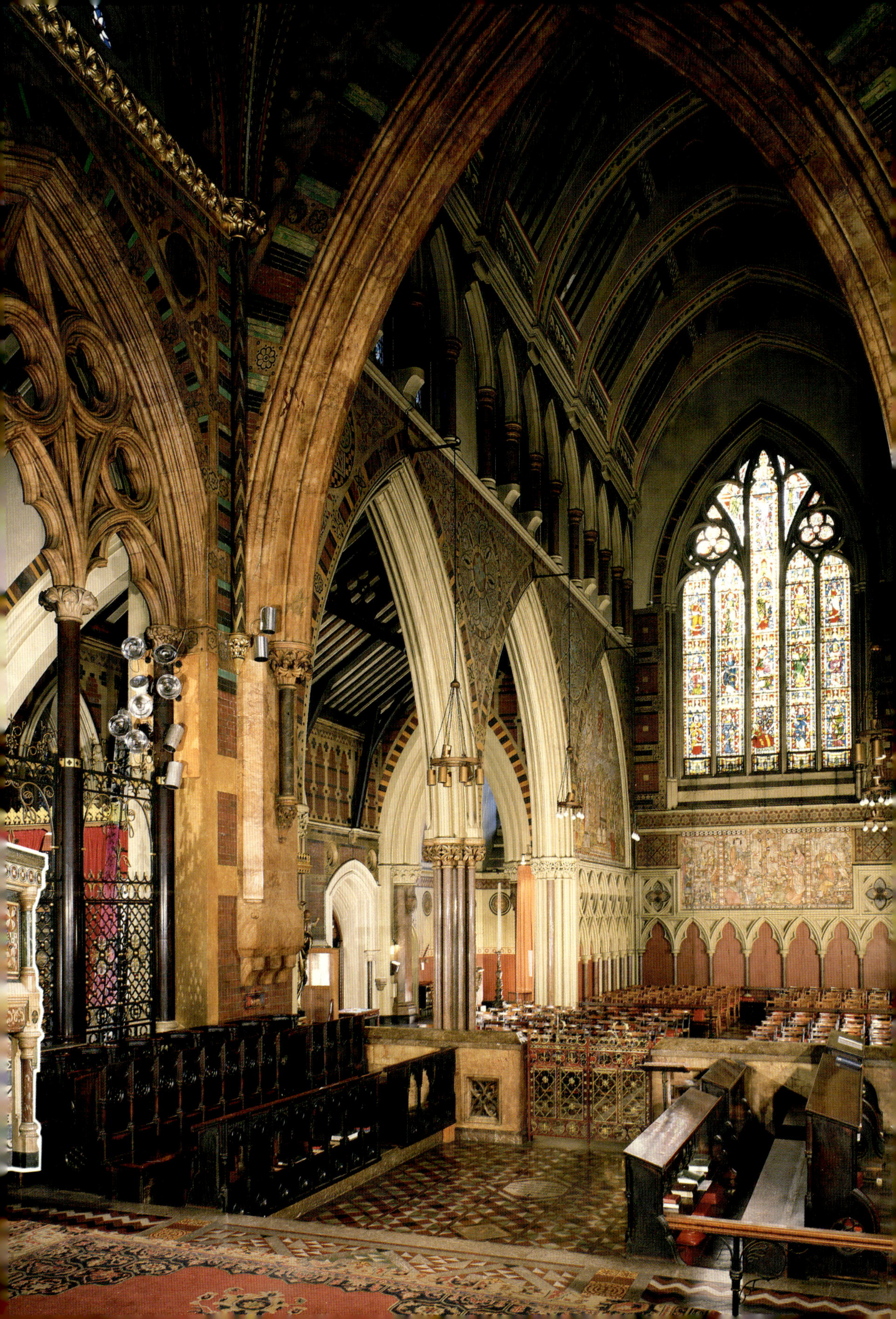

TO THE GLORY OF GOD IN MEMORY OF WILLIAM UPT

N·RICHARDS·FIRST·VICAR·OF·THIS·PARISH·A·D·1873

TO THE GLORY OF GOD AND IN MEMORY OF THE INCUMBENCY OF THE REV. BERDMORE COMPTON VICAR OF THIS PARISH FROM AD 1856

The Tiling

The tile paintings on the north wall date from 1873, and were erected in memory of Upton Richards, the first vicar, at a cost of £1,100. The tiles were designed by Butterfield to replace his original geometrical decoration. They were painted by Alexander Gibbs and manufactured by Henry Poole and Sons. The first panel on the left features the figures of Abel, Noah, Abraham, Moses, Miriam and Aaron; the second panel has David, Elijah, Jeremiah, Ezekiel, Daniel and St. John the Baptist. The centre panel has a representation of the Nativity which, as one commentator said, has all the tender simplicity of *Away in a Manger*. The fourth panel has figures of St Stephen, St Paul, St John, St Bartholomew, St Mary Magdalene and St Catherine. The final panel shows St Luke, St Peter, St Andrew, St Margaret, St Boniface and St Lawrence.

Below the west window, reflecting its theme, are three Old Testament scenes erected in 1889; Moses lifting up the serpent – symbolizing the Crucifixion; Abraham offering his only son, Isaac, as God gave his Son for our sins; and Melchizedek, priest of God – an archetype of Christ, the great High Priest. The last picture, put up in 1891 on the north wall of the tower, depicts the Ascension. James Stevens Curl describes how, in the decades after the completion of All Saints, Butterfield endeavoured in various ways to 'fine tune' the details of his masterpiece – and it is in that light that these decorative additions should be assessed.

RIGHT: *A detail from the original tiling behind the high altar, normally concealed by seasonal hangings.*

OPPOSITE: *The west end of the church. The original decoration in the arched spaces survives under 20th-century paint. Above a memorial tile painting is the great Jesse window.*

PREVIOUS PAGES: *Section of the tile painting from the north wall depicting the Nativity.*

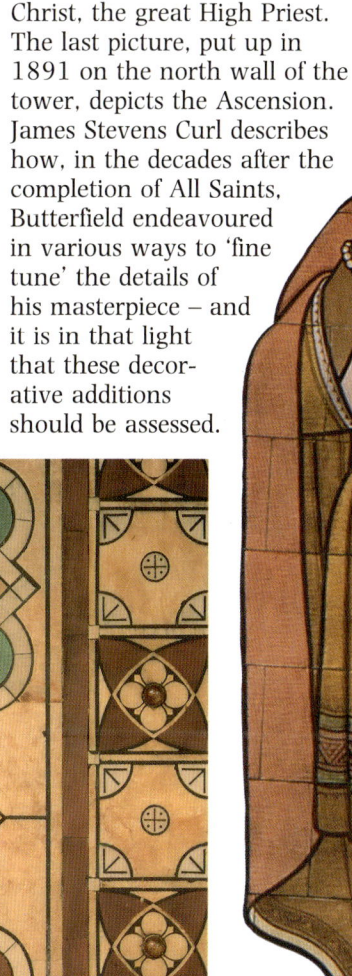

BELOW: *Detail from the tile painting on the north wall depicting one of the three kings from the Nativity.*

Decorative Features

The disagreements between Butterfield and his patron, Beresford-Hope, have been mentioned earlier. The complicated story of the stained glass at All Saints gives us some idea of the antagonism involved. Beresford-Hope intended that the work should be done by the Frenchman Henri Gerente. But M. Gerente died in 1849, and was succeeded by his brother Alfred. Alfred's glass, installed between 1853 and 1858, was generally agreed to be a failure. In particular his west window, based on the Tree of Jesse window at Wells Cathedral, was badly drawn, with too much yellow and dark green glass. Butterfield referred to its 'cabbage green' colour. Beresford-Hope initially refused to have it changed. He complained that Butterfield was 'fanatical in colour doctrines ... [he] gets more and more wild, and will not stop till he finds himself Butterfield against the world'. Eventually, in 1877, the glass was replaced by another Wells-inspired Jesse window, this time by Alexander Gibbs, in collaboration with Butterfield.

Gerente's glass in the south aisle was replaced in the late 1860s with windows again by Gibbs under Butterfield's supervision.

The glass in the clerestory is by Michael O'Connor and dates from 1853. *The Building News* remarked that 'the pure grey or grisaille effect is combined with a brilliant arrangement of jewelled colour.' More prosaically it has also been said that the windows resemble royalty in a pack of playing cards! The glass in the east window of the south chancel aisle is also O'Connor's work. It depicts Christ in majesty with St Edward and St Augustine.

The wooden screen, a somewhat incongruous 1962 addition at the end of the south aisle, is by Laurence King. It bears the figures of people who, as well as playing a distinctive part in the catholic revival in the Church of England, were associated with the early days of All Saints and its parish. They are: Dr Pusey, William Upton Richards, Harriet Brownlow Byron, Richard Benson (founder of the Society of St John the Evangelist) and Edward King, the saintly Bishop of Lincoln.

The serene statue of Our Lady with the Christ child was carved in Bruges by Louis Grosse and, after being painted and gilded in London, was presented to All Saints in 1924.

One of the great treasures of All Saints is the Lady Chapel, designed by Sir Ninian Comper in a late Gothic style and completed in 1911. The altar was commissioned by Father Henry Mackay. The chapel was enlarged in 1971 by Ian Grant as a memorial to Kenneth Ross (1908–1970), eighth vicar of All Saints (1957–69).

RIGHT: *The Lady Chapel designed by Sir Ninian Comper in 1911. The reredos is of Caen stone and alabaster, and shows the Virgin and Child surrounded by angels and saints. With the tester, it was restored by Peter Larkworthy in 1978–80.*

BELOW: *A window at the west end of the north aisle, showing the prophets Enoch, Isaiah and Malachi. It is possibly the only surviving piece of Gerente's work in All Saints, although it differs in style from his other known work.*

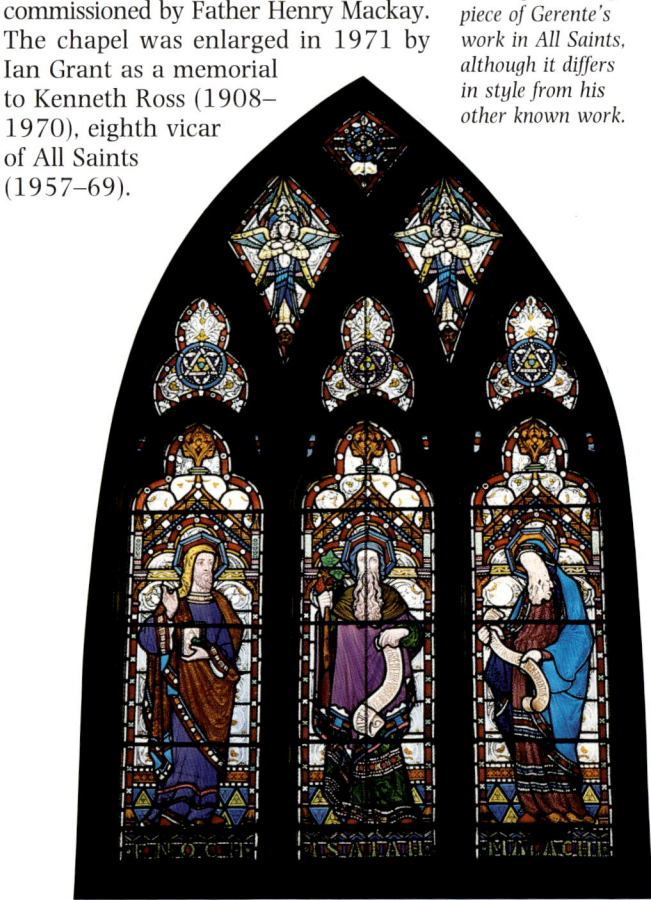

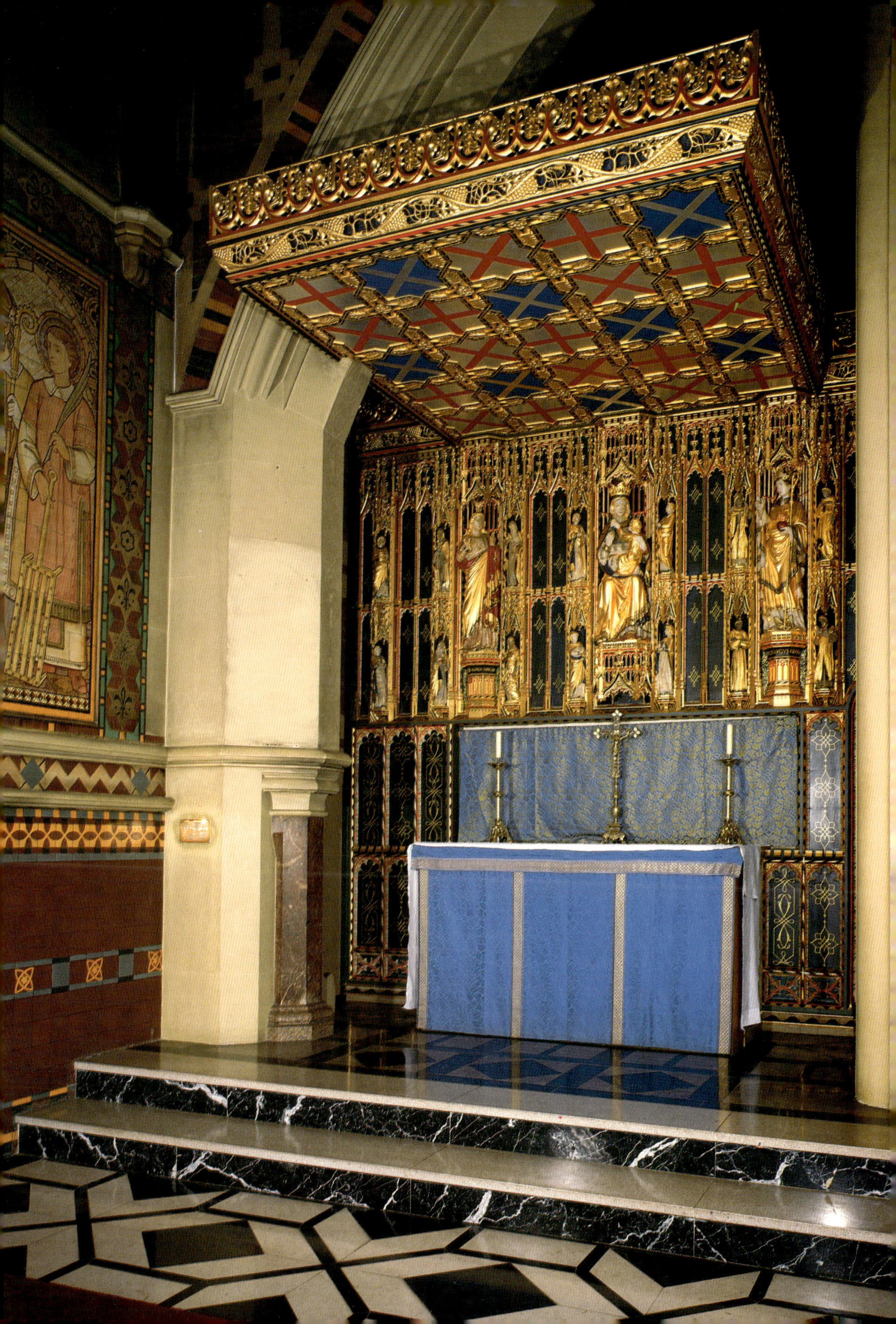

The Chancel and Sanctuary

Despite the restricted site, Butterfield dedicated almost one-third of the length of the church to the chancel, thus fulfilling the Tractarian requirement that the Sacraments should be stressed above the Word. To emphasise the importance of the chancel, the decoration becomes progressively richer towards the east. The abstract patterns of the nave give way to the gilded and painted decoration of the sanctuary. One enters the chancel through a pair of gilt iron and brass gates designed by Butterfield and made by Potter of South Molton Street, the Ecclesiological Society's favourite metalworker. The gates are set into a magnificent low screen of alabaster and marble. Butterfield intended it to be higher, but the Bishop of London (A.C. Tait) objected, and Beresford-Hope arranged a compromise. He viewed as deeply heretical Butterfield's suggestion that the Sacraments could perhaps be received outside the screen.

Inside the chancel, the side arches are filled with rich Decorated tracery modelled in alabaster and supported on red serpentine shafts. The elaborate floor echoes this richness with patterns of tiles in six colours. The vault, although influenced by 13th-century English work, has elements derived from the upper church of S. Francesco at Assisi. The ribs spring from capitals and wall shafts based on examples at Warmington church in Northamptonshire. Butterfield originally wanted an unpainted vault, with emphasis placed on the contrast between the alabaster ribs and the grey and white chalk infill. Beresford-Hope, however, favoured a painted ceiling and persuaded William Dyce to colour the vault at the same time (1853–9) as he worked on the great reredos. The vault was repainted by Comper in 1909, and by Larkworthy in 1978–80.

Nearby buildings prevented the glazing of the east end so Dyce's fresco, inspired by 15th-century Italian work, had to combine the functions of a medieval reredos and east window. Beresford-Hope called it 'a piece of success unlooked for and surprising' and claimed that it had been his suggestion. A large gap was left between the top of the altar and the bottom of the reredos because there was doubt whether a full-sized screen would be built, and Dyce was anxious that the lowest tier should be visible from the nave.

Unfortunately, the sulphurous London air soon harmed Dyce's reredos. What we see today is a fairly faithful copy that Comper painted in 1909 on wooden panels in front of the original. In the lower and middle sections, Christ's earthly life is depicted, while the upper section shows Christ in glory. The stiff figures in the lower sections contrast with the free movement of the figures surrounding Christ. In 1914 Comper used the four panels on the side walls of the sanctuary to represent the Greek and Latin Doctors of the Church. Above them are 16 boy and girl saints. This was also included in Larkworthy's 1978–80 restoration.

BELOW: *The chancel screen, designed by Butterfield in Derbyshire alabaster and various marbles. The visual gap which the low screen created between the top of the altar and the base of the reredos was filled with elaborate tiling, now normally covered.*

LEFT: *Comper's panel on the north wall of the sanctuary, depicting the Latin Doctors: (left to right) St Jerome, St Ambrose, St Augustine of Hippo, St Gregory the Great.*

The sanctuary, as originally conceived, was simply furnished. Butterfield was suspicious of ritualism, and subscribed to the Privy Council decision of 1857 that altars should be of wood and crosses be allowed only behind the altar, not on it. A gilt Maltese cross was fastened to the east wall, and the altar furnished with two candlesticks, two flower vases and a gospel book. Today's sanctuary furnishings were mostly acquired in the early years of the 20th century. Of particular importance is the great silver pyx, designed by Comper and given by the Duke of Newcastle in 1928 as a memorial to choristers killed in the First World War.

The organ is a superb four-manual instrument with 65 speaking stops, built by Harrison and Harrison in 1910 to a specification drawn up by Dr Walter Vale. It retains the best of the pipe work of its predecessor, the original and considerably smaller Hill organ. It is particularly interesting as it is the only large organ in London by Arthur Harrison which remains virtually in its original state. Notable for the beauty of its choir stops, it is a superb instrument for accompaniment; it is also skilfully voiced for the building. Though as big as those found in most cathedrals, it is perfectly tailored to the space afforded by the building. Without ever seeming to overpower, its sound is exciting and dynamic.

The rebuilding of the organ by Harrisons in 1957 included the provision of modern electro-pneumatic action and the replacement of a venerable hydraulic system by electric blowers. The Solo Tuba was added in 1971 as a memorial to Dr Vale.

ABOVE: *The Induction service of the Revd David Hutt in 1986. Above the High Altar is the 9 feet high silver tabernacle. The pyx containing the Reserved Sacrament formerly was lowered by an electric motor but is now operated manually.*

Historical Notes

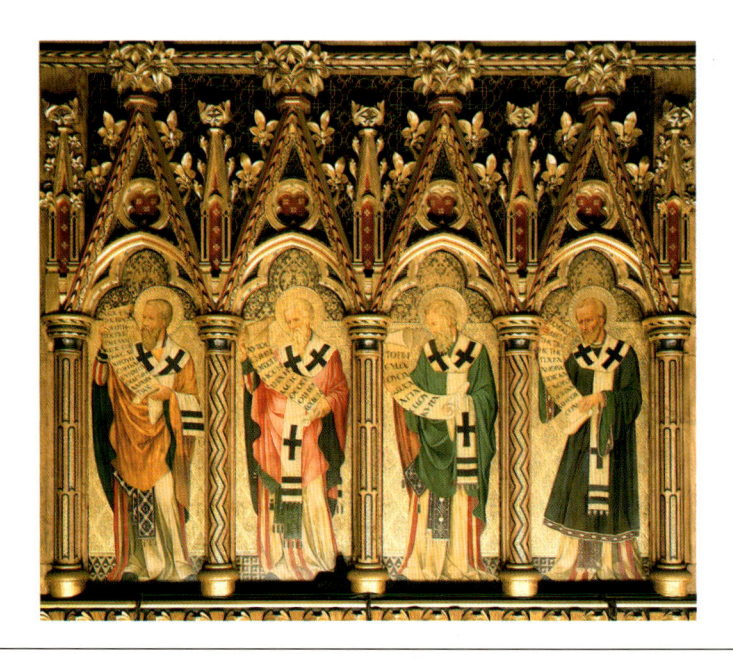

The Society of All Saints (Sisters of the Poor)

William Upton Richards (1811–1873), the first vicar (1868–73), played an important role in the establishment of the society in 1851. Under his direction, the foundress, Harriet Brownlow Byron, began to keep a definite rule of life. After training as a nurse, she began work in the slums which made up the area between Margaret Street and Oxford Street. The sisters occupied every building from 82, Margaret Street, All Saints House, up to Great Titchfield Street, providing a hospital, orphanage and convalescent home. After a move to new premises at London Colney, the Society has established its mother house in Oxford. Today, three sisters maintain a presence at No. 82.

The Institute of Christian Studies

The Butterfield building at No. 84, once the parish school rooms and clergy house, now houses the Institute of Christian Studies. This was founded by Michael Marshall (now Bishop) in 1970. This centre for adult education ceased to function in 1979 but reopened in 1988 with Dr John Cullen as Director.

The residential choir school

The choir school was established in 1856 and closed in 1968. Boys' voices have now been replaced by sopranos and the standard set by the professional singers is of the highest order, under the Director of Music and Organist, Harry Bramma, also Director of the Royal School of Church Music. Despite its small size when compared with its cathedral and university counterparts, its reputation was always in the first rank. It was the only parish choir school invited to provide boys to sing at the coronations of Edward VII, George V and VI, as well as Victoria's Jubilees. Many distinguished musicians started their careers at the School, but its most well known old boy was Laurence Olivier, who made his debut in a School production of *The Taming of the Shrew* at Stratford in 1922.

Envoi

All Saints was the pioneer building of the High Victorian phase of the Gothic Revival. The innovative, lavish use of colour and the uncompromising reference to a past style have provoked opinions ranging from loathing to love. The great Gothic revivalist and former churchwarden, G.E. Street, declared that 'this church is not only the most beautiful, but the most vigorous, thoughtful and original among them all'.

But perhaps the last word ought to go to John Ruskin: 'It is the first piece of architecture I have seen, built in modern days, which is free from all signs of timidity or incapacity . . . it challenges fearless comparison with the noblest work of any time. Having done this, we may do anything; there need be no limits to our hope or our confidence.'

ABOVE LEFT: *The panel on the south wall of the sanctuary, depicting the Greek Doctors: (left to right) St Gregory Naziansus, St Athanasius, St Basil, St John Chrysostom.*

RIGHT: *An historic etching of the Baptistery. The elaborate oak font cover, suspended by a wrought-iron frame, was removed early in the 20th century.*

Note

This guide has necessarily to cover a wide range of matters associated with All Saints. It has been decided with regret that space does not admit descriptions or illustrations of things generally unavailable for visitors to see. There are therefore no detailed accounts of vestments, plate and archives, but it should be noted that from time to time special tours are arranged.

Vicars of All Saints

William Upton Richards 1845–1873
(1811–1873)
Minister of the Margaret Chapel 1845–1849
Incumbent of All Saints 1849–1868
Vicar of All Saints 1868–1873

Berdmore Compton 1873–1886
(1820–1908)

William Allen Whitworth 1886–1905
(1840–1905)

George Frederick Holden 1905–1908
(1858–1908)

Henry Falconar Barclay Mackay 1908–1934
(1864–1936)

William Dudley Clements 1934–1942
(Dom Bernard Clements OSB)
(1890–1942)

Cyril Edric Tomkinson 1943–1951
(1886–1968)

Kenneth Needham Ross 1951–1969
(1908–1970)

Michael Eric Marshall 1969–1975
(1936–)

David Alan Sparrow 1976–1981
(1936–1981)

David Michael Hope 1982–1985
(1940–)

David Handley Hutt 1986–
(1938–)

Biographies of the vicars of All Saints are the subject of *Good and Faithful Servants* by Peter Galloway and Christopher Rawll, with a foreword by the Archbishop of Canterbury, published by Churchman Publishing Ltd.

All Saints Church
7 Margaret Street
London W1N 8JQ
Tel. 071 636 1788 or 071 636 9961

ABOVE: *Detail depicting three shepherds taken from the tile painting on the north wall.*